FROM SILENCE TO SOUND

A CULTURAL AND HISTORICAL STUDY OF INDIAN CINEMA

DR. JAGADEESH PILLAI

|| Dedicated to all wisdom seekers around the World ||

৪৩

Contents

Contents

Prayer

**"Om Bhadram Karnebhih Shrunuyaama
DevaahBhadram Pashyemaakshabhiryajatraah
SthirairangaistushtuvaamsastanoobhihVyashema
Devahitam YadaayuhSwasti Na Indro
VridhashravaahSwasti Nah Pooshaa
VishwavedaahSwasti Nastaarkshyo ArishtanemihSwasti
No Brihaspatir DadhaatuOm Shantih, Shantih, Shantih"**

The literal meaning of this mantra is: OM. O Gods! Let us
hear auspicious words from our ears. O reverent Gods! Let
us behold propitious visions from our eyes, let our organs
and body be stable, healthy, and strong. Let us do that
which is pleasing to the gods in the life span allotted to us.
May Indra, inscribed in the scriptures, bring us fortune!
May Pushan, the knower of the world, grant us prosperity!
May Trakshya, who vanquishes enemies, bestow us with
blessings! May Brihaspati bring us success!
OM Peace, Peace, Peace.

About The Author

Dr. Jagadeesh Pillai is a renowned Guinness World Record holder, writer, and researcher hailing from Varanasi, also known as the abode of Lord Shiva. With a Ph.D. in Vedic Science and a range of creative ideas and achievements, he is a true polymath. He is the author of more than 100 books including Research Publications. Although his roots can be traced back to Kerala, the people of Varanasi hold him in high regard and affectionately consider him one of their own.

In 1998, Dr. Pillai was offered a job at Banaras Hindu University, but he left the position after only two months to pursue greater goals in life. He believed that in order to study Indian scriptures and engage in other creative endeavours, he needed to retire from the daily grind of working solely for money at a young age.

He started an export business from scratch, using the knowledge he had gained from a previous job in the industry. His intelligence and unique approach to business led to great success in a short period of time, earning him more in just a decade and a half than he would have in a lifetime working in a government job. Upon the passing of Dr. APJ Abdul Kalam, Dr. Pillai decided to leave the business and dedicate himself to reading, studying, researching, and experimenting.

During his tenure in the export business, Dr. Pillai traveled to over 16 countries, gaining valuable insight and experiencing the world and life in detail.

Dr. Pillai has achieved four Guinness World Records in the following subjects:

"Script to Screen" - In this record, Dr. Pillai produced and directed an animation film within the shortest time possible, breaking the previous record set by Canadians. He has also received numerous national and international awards and recognitions for this achievement.

Longest Line of Postcards - For this record, Dr. Pillai created a line of 16,300 postcards on the occasion of the 163rd anniversary of Indian Postal Day. The event also included a questionnaire about the Indian flag.

Largest Poster Awareness Campaign - Dr. Pillai designed an awareness campaign on the subject of "Beti Bachao - Beti Padhao" (Save the Girl Child - Educate the Girl Child) to achieve this record.

Largest Envelope - In tribute to the Indian Prime Minister's "Make in India" initiative, Dr. Pillai created a 4000 square meter envelope using waste paper to achieve this record.

Attempted - **70000 Candles on a 210 kg Cake** - To celebrate the 70th Indian Independence Day, Dr. Pillai attempted to light 70,000 candles on a 210 kg cake, which was recorded in World Records India.

Attempted - **Documentary on Dhamek Stupa of Sarnath in 17 Languages** - Dr. Pillai attempted to create a documentary on the Dhamek Stupa of Sarnath, dubbing it in 17 different languages. The result of this attempt is currently awaiting confirmation from the Guinness World Records.

Dr. Pillai is skilled in teaching the Bhagavad Gita, a Hindu scripture, and is popular among young people. He has helped many young people improve their lives through his motivational teachings.

In addition to teaching, he has composed and sung numerous Sanskrit Bhajans and patriotic songs.

He has also written and directed several short films and documentaries for awareness campaigns, and has volunteered with the police in both UP and Kerala to spread awareness about various issues through videos and photography.

Incredibly, he has produced and directed over 100 documentaries about the city of Varanasi, all on his own.

He has also helped and guided more than 25 boys and girls to achieve world records through creative and innovative methods. He is a multifaceted person who uses his intellect and the blessings given to him by God to excel in various areas. He is both a teacher and a student, always learning and teaching, and is able to master any subject he comes across.

He is a selfless social activist and motivational speaker who has overcome struggles and failures to become a successful and enthusiastic individual with a rich life experience.

In addition to his work with the Bhagavad Gita, he is also an efficient Tarot card reader, Astro-Vastu consultant, and a talented singer and composer. He has sung the entire Ram Charita Manas and Bhagavad Gita in his own compositions, and has sung the phrase "Lokah Samastha Sukhino Bhavantu" in 50 different languages. He is currently working on a detailed and scientific study of Vedas, Upanishads, Puranas, and the Bhagavad Gita. He has also composed and sung the Hanuman Chalisa and Gayatri Mantra in 108 and 1008 different compositions, respectively.

Awards - Four Times Guinness World Records, Winner of Mahatma Gandhi Vishwa Shanti Puraskar, Mahatma Gandhi Global Peace Ambassador, Kashi Ratna Award, Dr. APJ Abdul Kalam Motivational Person of the Year 2017, Mother Teresa Award, Indira Gandhi Priyadarshini Award, Bharat Vikas Ratna Award, Udyog Ratna Award, Vigyan Prasar Award, Poorvanchal Ratn Samman.

PREFACE

As an avid moviegoer, I have been fascinated by the Indian film industry for many years. I have studied the history, culture, and artistic expression of Indian cinema with an enthusiasm that has only grown as I've watched more and more movies. My goal for this book, The Indian Film Industry: A Cultural and Historical Overview of Indian Cinema, is to share this enthusiasm with readers by providing an in-depth look at one of the most vibrant and influential film industries in the world.

This book is intended to serve as an introduction to the Indian film industry for readers who are new to the subject. It explores the evolution of Indian cinema from its early beginnings in the silent era to the modern-day blockbuster. The book covers various topics, including the development of different genres, the emergence of popular stars, and the impact of censorship on Indian cinema. It also examines the economics of the Indian film industry and explores how technological and societal changes have shaped its evolution.

The book draws on research from a variety of sources, including interviews with key figures in the Indian film industry, archival materials, and cultural analysis. I have also conducted extensive field research in India, including attending screenings, interviewing film-makers, and visiting locations associated with the production of Indian films. Through this research, I hope to provide readers with a comprehensive understanding of the Indian film industry and its various components.

I am deeply passionate about the art of Indian cinema and hope that this book will help to spread the appreciation of this wonderful art form. I believe that Indian cinema has a great deal to offer to the world and I am excited to share its cultural and historical significance with my readers.

I

Introduction to Indian Cinema

Indian cinema is one of the largest and most influential film industries in the world. With its diverse culture, languages, and storytelling traditions, it has captivated audiences for over a century. From the silent era to the present day, Indian cinema has undergone remarkable transformations, both technically and aesthetically. This chapter provides an overview of the history and evolution of Indian cinema, from its beginnings to its current status as a major global film industry.

The Early Years of Indian Cinema (1913-1930)

The birth of Indian cinema can be traced back to 1913, with the release of Raja Harishchandra, directed by Dadasaheb Phalke. This silent film marked the beginning of the Indian film industry, which would go on to become one of the largest in the world. The early years of Indian cinema were marked by the production of mythological and historical films, as well as social dramas and comedies. These films were usually accompanied by live music and sound effects, and were well-received by audiences.

The Golden Age of Indian Cinema (1940s-1960s)

The 1940s and 1950s are considered the Golden Age of Indian cinema. This period was marked by the emergence of some of India's most talented actors, directors, and filmmakers. The films produced during this time were characterized by their use of song and dance, as well as their social and political commentary. Themes such as national identity, freedom, and class struggle were explored in films such as Awaara, Shree 420, and Mother India. This period also saw the emergence of Bollywood, a term used to describe the Mumbai-based Hindi film industry.

The New Indian Cinema (1970s-1980s)

The 1970s and 1980s saw a major shift in Indian cinema, with the emergence of the New Indian Cinema movement. This period was characterized by a rejection of the traditional conventions of Indian cinema, and a new emphasis on realism and social commentary. The films produced during this time were marked by their use of non-linear narratives, unconventional storytelling techniques, and a focus on the lives of ordinary people. This period also saw the emergence of regional cinemas, such as the Bengali and Malayalam film industries, which produced films that were both critically acclaimed and commercially successful.

The Contemporary Indian Cinema (1990s-Present)

In the 1990s and 2000s, Indian cinema underwent major changes, with the emergence of new technologies and the globalization of the film industry. The use of special effects, digital editing, and digital cameras revolutionized the way Indian films were made and marketed. This period also saw the emergence of a new generation of filmmakers who used technology to tell stories in new and innovative ways. The contemporary Indian film industry is now characterized by a vibrant and diverse range of films, including commercial blockbusters, independent films, and regional productions.

Indian cinema has come a long way since its beginnings in 1913. Today, it is a major global film industry, with a rich history and a diverse range of films that reflect the country's cultural, social, and political landscape. From the silent era to the present day, Indian cinema has undergone major transformations, both technically and aesthetically, and continues to captivate audiences around the world. The story of Indian cinema is a story of innovation, creativity, and cultural expression, and its impact on the world of film is sure to continue for many years to come.

*"Indian films have the power to move people
not just emotionally, but also spiritually."*

– Karan Johar

৪৩

II

Evolution and Development of Indian Cinema

Indian cinema has undergone a number of significant transformations since its birth in 1913. From its early days as a fledgling film industry to its current status as one of the largest and most influential in the world, Indian cinema has evolved and developed in countless ways. This chapter explores the key phases of development in Indian cinema, from its early beginnings to the present day, and examines the technological, aesthetic, and cultural factors that have shaped the evolution of this fascinating art form.

The Silent Era (1913-1931)

The earliest days of Indian cinema were marked by the production of silent films. These films were often adaptations of traditional Indian stories and legends, and were usually accompanied by live music and sound effects. Despite their limited technical capabilities, these films were popular with audiences and helped to lay the foundation for the Indian film industry.

The Talkie Era (1931-1940s)

The advent of sound technology in the 1930s marked the beginning of a new era in Indian cinema. The first "talkie" film was released in 1931, and quickly gained popularity with audiences. The integration of sound into Indian films brought about new possibilities for storytelling, as well as new challenges for filmmakers. The use of song and dance became an integral part of the Indian film experience, and musicals emerged as a popular genre.

The Golden Age of Indian Cinema (1940s-1960s)

The 1940s and 1950s are considered the Golden Age of Indian cinema. During this time, Indian filmmakers produced a number of critically acclaimed and commercially successful films that explored social and political issues and reflected the country's cultural identity. These films were characterized by their use of song and dance, as well as their powerful storytelling and dynamic cinematography. The emergence of Bollywood as a major film industry during this period helped to cement the place of Indian cinema on the global stage.

The New Indian Cinema (1970s-1980s)

The 1970s and 1980s saw a major shift in Indian cinema, with the emergence of the New Indian Cinema movement.

This period was characterized by a rejection of the traditional conventions of Indian cinema, and a new emphasis on realism and social commentary. The films produced during this time were marked by their use of non-linear narratives, unconventional storytelling techniques, and a focus on the lives of ordinary people. The New Indian Cinema movement also helped to spur the growth of regional cinemas, such as the Bengali and Malayalam film industries, which produced films that were both critically acclaimed and commercially successful.

The Contemporary Indian Cinema (1990s-Present)

In the 1990s and 2000s, Indian cinema underwent major changes, with the emergence of new technologies and the globalization of the film industry. The use of special effects, digital editing, and digital cameras revolutionized the way Indian films were made and marketed. This period also saw the emergence of a new generation of filmmakers who used technology to tell stories in new and innovative ways. The contemporary Indian film industry is now characterized by a vibrant and diverse range of films, including commercial blockbusters, independent films, and regional productions.

"Indian films are like a big family and I'm proud to be a part of it."

– Aishwarya Rai

III

Themes in Indian Cinema

Indian cinema is renowned for its rich and diverse storytelling, which reflects the cultural, social, and political complexities of Indian society. Over the years, Indian filmmakers have explored a wide range of themes and subject matter, from romance and family drama to social and political commentary. In this chapter, we will explore some of the key themes that have emerged in Indian cinema over the years and examine how these themes have reflected the changing social and cultural landscape of India.

Romance and Family Drama

One of the most enduring themes in Indian cinema is the portrayal of romantic love and family relationships. From the early days of Indian cinema to the present day, filmmakers have explored the complexities of love and family life, often set against the backdrop of India's cultural and social norms. The portrayal of love and family relationships in Indian cinema has often reflected the changing attitudes towards these themes over the years, with filmmakers exploring both traditional and more progressive views.

Social and Political Commentary

Another major theme in Indian cinema is the exploration of social and political issues. Indian filmmakers have long used their art form as a means of addressing important social and political issues, such as poverty, gender discrimination, and political corruption. The portrayal of these issues in Indian cinema has often reflected the broader political and social context of the country, and has helped to raise awareness and spark discussions about these important topics.

Religion and Spirituality

Religion and spirituality have long been important themes in Indian cinema, reflecting the rich religious and spiritual traditions of the country. Indian filmmakers have explored the complexities of religious and spiritual life in India, often using these themes as a means of exploring broader questions about the nature of existence, the meaning of life, and the place of spirituality in a rapidly changing world.

Identity and Culture

Identity and culture are key themes in Indian cinema, reflecting the country's diverse cultural and linguistic heritage. Indian filmmakers have used the medium of cinema to explore questions of cultural identity, particularly in the context of India's rapidly changing society. Through their work, they have sought to explore the tensions between tradition and modernity, and the ways in which cultural identity is shaped by historical, social, and political factors.

Regionalism

Finally, regionalism is an important theme in Indian cinema, reflecting the rich linguistic and cultural diversity of the country. Regional cinemas, such as the Bengali and Malayalam film industries, have produced a wealth of films that explore the unique cultural and linguistic traditions of their respective regions. These films have helped to celebrate the diversity of Indian culture and to promote a greater understanding of the country's linguistic and cultural heritage.

The themes explored in Indian cinema are diverse and complex, reflecting the rich cultural and social landscape of the country. From the portrayal of romantic love and family relationships to the exploration of social and political issues, Indian filmmakers have used their art form to address a wide range of themes and subject matter. Through their work, they have helped to shape the cultural and social discourse of India and to shed light on some of the most important issues facing the country today. The continued exploration of these themes in Indian cinema is sure to be an important part of the ongoing story of this rich and dynamic art form.

"Indians films are a reflection of our culture,
our diversity, and our values."

– Aamir Khan

୫

IV

Indian Cinematographers and Directors

Indian cinema has a rich history of talented and innovative cinematographers and directors, who have helped to shape the course of the industry over the years. From the early days of Indian cinema to the present day, these filmmakers have used their creative vision and technical skills to bring a wide range of stories and themes to life on the big screen. In this chapter, we will examine some of the key figures in Indian cinema and explore their contributions to the development and evolution of this rich and dynamic art form.

Cinematographers

Cinematographers play a crucial role in shaping the visual look and feel of a film. They work closely with the director to bring the story to life, using a range of techniques, including lighting, camera movement, and special effects, to create the desired visual style. Indian cinematographers have a long history of innovation and creativity, and have played a key role in shaping the visual style of Indian cinema over the years.

Some of the most prominent and influential Indian cinematographers include V.K. Murthy, who was one of the first Indian cinematographers to work in the Indian film industry and is widely credited with helping to establish the visual style of Indian cinema. Murthy's work was characterized by his use of vivid colors and bold camera movements, and he was known for his innovative use of light and shadow to create a range of moods and emotions in his films.

Another important figure in Indian cinematography is Subrata Mitra, who was a key member of the Satyajit Ray film team and is widely regarded as one of the greatest cinematographers in Indian cinema. Mitra's work was characterized by his use of natural light and his emphasis on visual storytelling, and he was known for his ability to create a range of moods and emotions through his use of light and shadow.

Directors

Directors are the creative visionaries behind Indian cinema, responsible for bringing stories to life on the big screen. Indian cinema has a long history of talented and innovative directors, who have explored a wide range of themes and subject matter over the years. From the early days of Indian cinema to the present day, Indian directors have used their creative vision and technical skills to create films that have captivated audiences around the world.

One of the most important figures in Indian cinema is Satyajit Ray, who is widely regarded as one of the greatest filmmakers of all time. Ray's films were characterized by their rich and complex storytelling, and his use of visual storytelling to explore themes of human relationships, identity, and spirituality. Ray's films had a profound impact on Indian cinema and helped to establish the country as a major player in the world of filmmaking.

Another influential figure in Indian cinema is Bimal Roy, who was one of the most important directors of the Indian New Wave and is widely regarded as one of the greatest filmmakers of his generation. Roy's films were characterized by their powerful social commentary, and his use of visual storytelling to explore complex themes such as poverty, gender discrimination, and political corruption.

Indian cinematographers and directors have played a crucial role in the development and evolution of Indian cinema over the years. From the early days of Indian cinema to the present day, these filmmakers have used their creative vision and technical skills to bring a wide range of stories and themes to life on the big screen. Their contributions have helped to shape the course of Indian cinema and to establish the country as a major player in the world of filmmaking. As Indian cinema continues to evolve and grow, these key figures will undoubtedly continue to play a central role in shaping the future of this rich and dynamic art form.

*"Indian films are a celebration of life, love
and hope."*

– Priyanka Chopra

୫

V

Music and Soundtracks in Indian Cinema

Music and sound play a critical role in Indian cinema, and the musical scores and soundtracks of Indian films are a testament to the rich musical heritage of the country. From the early days of Indian cinema to the present day, music has been used to evoke a wide range of emotions and to help bring the stories of Indian films to life. In this chapter, we will examine the role of music and sound in Indian cinema and explore the history and evolution of the Indian film soundtrack.

The Early Years of Indian Cinema

In the early days of Indian cinema, music and sound were used to accompany the silent films that dominated the industry. Music was typically played live by a small ensemble, and was used to underscore key moments in the film and to help to build atmosphere and tension. The music of these early films was typically rooted in classical Indian music, and was often used to evoke the cultural and historical heritage of the country.

The Transition to Sound

With the advent of sound technology, Indian cinema underwent a major transformation. The introduction of sound allowed filmmakers to create new and more sophisticated musical scores, and to explore a wider range of musical styles and genres. In the early sound films, music was used to help establish the mood and atmosphere of the film, and to provide a musical accompaniment to the dialogue and sound effects.

The Golden Age of Indian Cinema

The period from the 1950s to the 1970s is often referred to as the "Golden Age" of Indian cinema, and this was a time when music and sound played an increasingly important role in Indian films. This period saw the emergence of a new generation of talented composers and musicians, who created a range of innovative and original musical scores. The music of this period was characterized by its use of traditional Indian instruments and styles, combined with a variety of Western influences.

The Evolution of the Indian Film Soundtrack

In the decades since the Golden Age of Indian cinema, music and sound have continued to play a crucial role in

Indian films. Today, Indian filmmakers are using music and sound to create a wide range of musical scores and soundtracks, drawing on a wide range of musical styles and genres. The soundtracks of Indian films are now widely recognized as some of the most innovative and original in the world, and are widely sought after by fans of Indian cinema around the world.

Music and sound have played a critical role in Indian cinema from the early days of the industry to the present day. From classical Indian music to contemporary soundtracks, music has been used to evoke a wide range of emotions and to bring the stories of Indian films to life. As Indian cinema continues to evolve and grow, the musical scores and soundtracks of Indian films will undoubtedly continue to play a crucial role in shaping the future of this rich and dynamic art form.

"I am proud to be a part of an industry which has the power to bring people together."

– Shah Rukh Khan

VI
Genres of Indian Cinema

Indian cinema has a rich and diverse history, and over the years, Indian filmmakers have explored a wide range of genres and styles. From romantic comedies and drama to action-packed thrillers, Indian films have something to offer for every taste. In this chapter, we will examine the various genres of Indian cinema and explore the history and evolution of each genre.

Bollywood and Masala Films

Bollywood is the informal term used to describe the Hindi-language film industry, and it is one of the largest and most prolific film industries in the world. Bollywood is best known for its masala films, which are a unique blend of drama, romance, comedy, action, and music. These films often feature big-name stars, elaborate dance sequences, and soaring musical numbers, and they have become synonymous with Indian cinema around the world.

Art and Parallel Cinema

Art and parallel cinema is a term used to describe a more serious and realistic style of Indian filmmaking that emerged in the 1960s and 1970s. These films were characterized by their use of real-life themes and complex characters, and they often dealt with social and political issues in a more nuanced and sophisticated way than the typical Bollywood masala film. Art and parallel cinema helped to push the boundaries of Indian cinema and to explore new and innovative styles and genres.

Action and Thriller Films

Action and thriller films have been a staple of Indian cinema for many years, and these films often feature high-stakes action sequences, dramatic twists and turns, and larger-than-life characters. From the early days of Indian cinema to the present day, action and thriller films have remained popular with audiences, and they continue to be a major part of the Indian film industry.
b__+++

Drama and family films are a staple of Indian cinema, and these films often explore the relationships and dynamics of Indian families and communities. From heartwarming tales of family love and sacrifice to powerful dramas that delve into the complexities of Indian life, drama and family films have a broad appeal and have been popular with audiences for many years.

Indian cinema is a rich and diverse art form that has explored a wide range of genres and styles over the years. From the big-budget Bollywood masala films to the more serious and nuanced art and parallel cinema, Indian filmmakers have created a wealth of memorable and powerful films that have captivated audiences around the world. Whether you prefer action-packed thrills, heartwarming dramas, or something in between, Indian cinema has something for everyone.

"Indian films celebrate the beauty of our country and the strength of our culture."

– Amitabh Bachchan

VII
Popular Indian Film Stars

Indian cinema has produced some of the biggest and most beloved movie stars in the world, and these actors and actresses have helped to shape the history and evolution of Indian cinema. In this chapter, we will take a closer look at some of the most popular and influential Indian film stars and examine the impact that they have had on the Indian film industry.

Raj Kapoor

Raj Kapoor is considered one of the most influential figures in Indian cinema, and he is often referred to as the "Charlie Chaplin of Indian cinema." Kapoor was a legendary film director, producer, and actor, and his films, which often dealt with themes of poverty, social justice, and human dignity, helped to define the Hindi-language film industry. Kapoor was also known for his music, and his films often featured memorable and iconic songs that became part of the cultural fabric of India.

Dev Anand

Dev Anand was another legendary figure in Indian cinema, and he was one of the most popular and influential actors of the 1950s and 1960s. Anand appeared in more than 100 films, and his style and charisma helped to define the golden age of Indian cinema. Anand was known for his dashing good looks, energetic performances, and his ability to bring life and energy to his films.

Shah Rukh Khan

Shah Rukh Khan, also known as the "King of Bollywood," is one of the biggest and most popular stars in Indian cinema today. Khan has appeared in more than 80 films, and his versatility and natural acting ability have made him one of the most sought-after actors in the industry. Khan has won numerous awards for his work, and he continues to be one of the most influential and beloved figures in Indian cinema.

Amitabh Bachchan

Amitabh Bachchan is another legendary figure in Indian cinema, and he is considered one of the most important actors of his generation. Bachchan has appeared in more than 200 films, and his powerful performances and dynamic screen presence have earned him numerous awards and accolades. Bachchan has also been a trailblazer in Indian cinema, and his work has helped to pave the way for future generations of actors and filmmakers.

Madhuri Dixit

Madhuri Dixit is one of the most popular and beloved actresses in Indian cinema, and she has won numerous awards for her work in film. Dixit has appeared in more than 70 films, and her natural beauty and acting ability have made her a favorite with audiences around the world. Dixit is also known for her grace and poise, and she continues to be a major figure in Indian cinema.

Indian cinema has produced some of the biggest and most beloved movie stars in the world, and these actors and actresses have helped to shape the history and evolution of Indian cinema. Whether it is the legendary Raj Kapoor, the dashing Dev Anand, or the charismatic Shah Rukh Khan, Indian film stars have captivated audiences and earned their place in the pantheon of Indian cultural heroes. These actors and actresses continue to inspire new generations of filmmakers and to contribute to the rich and diverse history of Indian cinema.

*"Indian films have the power to make us
smile, laugh, and even cry."*

– Anil Kapoor

VIII
Regional Indian Film Industries

Indian cinema is a diverse and multifaceted industry, encompassing a range of regional film industries that reflect the rich cultural and linguistic heritage of India. In this chapter, we will explore some of the key regional film industries in India and examine the unique contributions that they have made to the history and evolution of Indian cinema.

Tamil Cinema

Tamil cinema is one of the oldest and most established regional film industries in India, and it has a rich history that dates back to the early 20th century. Tamil films are known for their strong cultural roots, and they often feature local music, dance, and storytelling traditions. Some of the most popular and influential Tamil films include M.G. Ramachandran's "Adimai Penn" (1969) and

Mani Ratnam's "Roja" (1992).

Telugu Cinema

Telugu cinema is the film industry of the Telugu-speaking region of India, and it is one of the largest film industries in India in terms of the number of films produced each year. Telugu films are known for their strong themes, memorable music, and engaging characters, and they often feature lavish production values and high-quality cinematography. Some of the most popular and influential Telugu films include "Annamayya" (1997) and "Magadheera" (2009).

Bengali Cinema

Bengali cinema is the film industry of the Bengali-speaking region of India, and it has a rich history that dates back to the 1930s. Bengali films are known for their artistic sensibility, and they often explore complex themes and ideas that challenge conventional wisdom. Some of the most popular and influential Bengali films include Satyajit Ray's "Pather Panchali" (1955) and Ritwik Ghatak's "Meghe Dhaka Tara" (1960).

Marathi Cinema

Marathi cinema is the film industry of the Marathi-speaking region of India, and it has a rich history that dates back to the silent film era. Marathi films are known for their cultural roots and their focus on social issues, and they often feature local music, dance, and storytelling traditions. Some of the most popular and influential Marathi films include "Shyamchi Aai" (1953) and "Sairat"

(2016).

Gujarati Cinema

Gujarati cinema is the film industry of the Gujarati-speaking region of India, and it has a rich history that dates back to the 1930s. Gujarati films are known for their musical scores, and they often feature local music, dance, and storytelling traditions. Some of the most popular and influential Gujarati films include "Rangilo Raaj" (1952) and "Kevi Rite Jaish" (2012).

Regional Indian film industries are an important part of the cultural and artistic heritage of India, and they have made significant contributions to the history and evolution of Indian cinema. Whether it is the cultural roots of Tamil cinema, the themes and ideas explored in Bengali cinema, or the music and dance of Gujarati cinema, regional Indian film industries are a testament to the rich and diverse cultural fabric of India. These film industries continue to thrive and to provide audiences with a unique and engaging form of entertainment that reflects the rich cultural and linguistic heritage of India.

"Indian films have the ability to capture the hearts and minds of audiences across the world."

– A.R. Rahman

IX

Censorship in Indian Cinema

Indian cinema has a long and complex relationship with censorship, with various forms of censorship affecting the production, distribution, and exhibition of films in India for much of its history. Censorship has had a significant impact on the evolution of Indian cinema, shaping the way that filmmakers tell their stories and influencing the themes and content of their films.

Early Censorship in India

Censorship in India has a long history, with the British colonial government imposing restrictions on the production and exhibition of Indian films from the early 20th century. The Indian Cinematograph Act of 1918 established the first official censorship system in India, giving the government broad powers to censor or ban films that were deemed to be offensive or harmful to public morality.

Post-Independence Censorship

After India gained independence in 1947, the censorship system was reformed, with the Indian Cinematograph Act of 1952 establishing a new set of guidelines for censorship in India. The new system gave the government the power to censor films on a wide range of grounds, including obscenity, violence, political content, and religious sentiments. This new censorship system was used to restrict or ban a number of films in the following years, including "Aandhi" (1975), "Fire" (1996), and "Water" (2005).

Contemporary Censorship in India

In recent years, censorship in India has come under increasing scrutiny, with many filmmakers and activists arguing that censorship restrictions are stifling the artistic freedom of filmmakers and limiting the ability of Indian cinema to tell a wide range of stories. The current censorship system in India is complex, with different regulations governing different forms of media, including film, television, and digital media. Despite the many challenges posed by censorship, Indian cinema continues to thrive, with filmmakers adapting and finding new ways to tell their stories in the face of censorship restrictions.

Impact of Censorship on Indian Cinema

Censorship has had a significant impact on the evolution of Indian cinema, shaping the way that filmmakers tell their stories and influencing the themes and content of their films. Many Indian filmmakers have been forced to adapt their storytelling techniques to work around censorship restrictions, using subtle and symbolic imagery to convey their messages. As a result, Indian cinema has become more nuanced and sophisticated over time, with filmmakers developing a range of creative strategies to tell their stories in the face of censorship restrictions.

Censorship has been a central issue in the history of Indian cinema, affecting the way that filmmakers tell their stories and influencing the themes and content of their films. Despite the many challenges posed by censorship, Indian cinema continues to thrive, with filmmakers adapting and finding new ways to tell their stories in the face of censorship restrictions. As Indian cinema continues to evolve, censorship will continue to play an important role in shaping the future of this vibrant and diverse industry.

"Indian films have a unique blend of art, music, and storytelling that make them so special."

– Madhuri Dixit

X

The Economics of Indian Cinema

Indian cinema is a multi-billion dollar industry, with a rich and diverse history that spans over a century. The economics of Indian cinema have undergone significant changes and transformations over the years, adapting to the changing demands and preferences of audiences, as well as to technological innovations and economic trends.

Early Years of Indian Cinema

In the early years of Indian cinema, the film industry was dominated by a small number of studios, which produced, distributed, and exhibited films. These studios controlled the entire value chain of the film industry, from production to distribution and exhibition. This vertical integration of the film industry allowed the studios to maximize their profits, while limiting the bargaining power of other industry players, such as filmmakers and actors.

The Rise of Bollywood

In the 1970s and 1980s, the Indian film industry underwent a major transformation, with the rise of Bollywood as the dominant film industry in India. Bollywood's success was driven by a combination of factors, including the popularity of musicals, the emergence of new stars, and the growing demand for Indian films around the world. As Bollywood grew, it became an increasingly important driver of the Indian economy, generating billions of dollars in revenue and providing employment for millions of people.

The Contemporary Film Industry

Today, the Indian film industry is a complex and diverse sector, with multiple regional film industries, as well as a thriving independent film sector. The economics of the film industry have been impacted by a range of factors, including the increasing competition from international films, the rise of digital distribution platforms, and the growing popularity of regional films. Despite these challenges, the Indian film industry remains one of the largest and most vibrant film industries in the world, with a rich tradition of storytelling and a vibrant culture of creativity and innovation.

The Importance of the Film Industry to the Indian Economy

The film industry is an important contributor to the Indian economy, providing employment and generating billions of dollars in revenue each year. The industry also has a number of indirect economic benefits, including the development of a vibrant entertainment sector, the growth of the tourism industry, and the creation of new business opportunities in areas such as advertising, merchandizing, and distribution. The film industry also plays a significant role in promoting Indian culture and values around the world, strengthening India's position as a major player in the global cultural arena.

The economics of Indian cinema have undergone significant changes and transformations over the years, adapting to the changing demands and preferences of audiences, as well as to technological innovations and economic trends. Despite the challenges posed by the rapidly changing landscape of the film industry, Indian cinema remains one of the largest and most vibrant film industries in the world, with a rich tradition of storytelling and a vibrant culture of creativity and innovation. As Indian cinema continues to evolve, it will remain an important contributor to the Indian economy and a major player in the global cultural arena.

*"Indian films are a celebration of diversity
and the power of the human spirit."*

– Sushmita Sen

ॐ

XI

The Impact of Indian Cinema on Society

Indian cinema has had a profound impact on Indian society, shaping and reflecting the values, beliefs, and attitudes of the country's people. Over the course of a century, Indian cinema has evolved and developed, adapting to changing cultural, social, and economic conditions, and reflecting the changing attitudes and values of Indian society.

Early Indian Cinema and Society

In the early years of Indian cinema, the film industry was largely dominated by the urban, English-speaking elite, and the films produced reflected their values and attitudes. The early films were often escapist in nature, depicting a romanticized view of India that was at odds with the realities of life in the country. Despite this, early Indian cinema did have a significant impact on society, introducing new ideas and values and serving as a powerful tool for social and political change.

The Emergence of Realistic Cinema

In the 1940s and 1950s, a new form of Indian cinema emerged, known as "realistic" or "social" cinema. This new type of film was characterized by a focus on social and political issues, and was intended to raise awareness and spark change. The realistic films of this era tackled a range of issues, including poverty, inequality, and corruption, and played a significant role in shaping public opinion and sparking social and political activism.

The Rise of Bollywood and Popular Culture

In the 1970s and 1980s, Bollywood emerged as the dominant film industry in India, and the films produced by the industry had a profound impact on Indian society. The Bollywood films of this era were characterized by their lavish production values, upbeat musical numbers, and romanticized view of love and relationships. The films and the stars that appeared in them became symbols of popular culture, influencing fashion, music, and social attitudes.

The Contemporary Film Industry and Society

Today, the Indian film industry is more diverse and fragmented than ever, reflecting the complex and multi-faceted nature of Indian society. The films produced by the industry continue to have a significant impact on Indian society, shaping attitudes, values, and beliefs. Indian cinema also reflects the social and political issues that are of concern to the country's people, and serves as a powerful tool for social and political activism.

Indian cinema has had a profound impact on Indian society, shaping and reflecting the values, beliefs, and attitudes of the country's people. Over the course of a century, Indian cinema has evolved and developed, adapting to changing cultural, social, and economic conditions, and reflecting the changing attitudes and values of Indian society. As Indian cinema continues to evolve, it will continue to have a significant impact on Indian society, serving as a powerful tool for social and political change, and reflecting the complex and multi-faceted nature of Indian life.

Other Books Of The Author

59. The Holistic Cow: A Look at the Physical, Spiritual, and Cultural Importance of Cows in India
60. Arts of Healing
61. Exploring the Divine
62. Understanding Five Elements
63. The Etymology of Ram
64. Symbols of India
65. Voice of Change (About Speeches of Great Men)
66. She Speaks (About Speeches of Great Women)
67. Patriotism on Celluloid – Brief About Patriotic Films
68. The Music of Motivation: A Brief Guide to Inspirational Film Songs
69. **Unlocking the Secrets of the Dashopanishads**
70. A Cultural Mosaic
71. Ancient Traditions, Modern Minds
72. Ecos of Ancient Wisdom
73. Beneath the Surface
74. From Temples to Ashrams
75. Sages of the Subcontinent
76. The Art of Healling (Ayurveda, Yoga & Naturopathy)
77. Indian Kitchen
78. The Festivals of India
79. The Indian Epics Retold
80. The Power of Mantras
81. The Indian River Ganges
82. The Indian Architecture
83. Rites of Passage
84. The Indian Silk Road
85. The Indian Literature
86. The Indian Villages
87. The Indian Folks & Crafts
88. The Way of Buddha
89. The Ramayan of Tulsidas

৳

Contact

DR. JAGADEESH PILLAI

MBA & PhD in Vedic Science

Four Times Guinness World Record Holder

Winner of Mahatma Gandhi Vishwa Shanti Puraskar and
Global Peace Ambassador

Gemology, Astro & Vastu Consultant - Spiritual Counselor

Consultant for designing World Record Ideas

Efficient Tarot Card Reader

9839093003

myrichindia@gmail.com

drjagadeeshpillai@facebook

drjagadeeshpillai@instagram
jagadeeshpillai@youtube

www. JAGADEESHPILLAI.com

౪

|| LOKAHA SAMASTHAHA SUKHINO BHAVANTU ||

ॐ